OUR
GRE★T
STATES

WHAT'S GREAT ABOUT
MISSISSIPPI?

✳ Anita Yasuda

LERNER PUBLICATIONS ✳ MINNEAPOLIS

CONTENTS

MISSISSIPPI
WELCOMES YOU! ✳ 4

Content Consultant: Deanne Stephens Nuwer,
PhD, Associate Professor of History, University
of Southern Mississippi

Lerner Publications Company
A division of Lerner Publishing Group, Inc.
241 First Avenue North
Minneapolis, MN 55401 USA

For reading levels and more information, look
up this title at www.lernerbooks.com.

Main body text set in ITC Franklin Gothic Std
Book Condensed 12/15.
Typeface provided by Adobe Systems.

Library of Congress Cataloging-in-Publication
Data

The Cataloging-in-Publication Data for *What's
Great about Mississippi?* is on file at the
Library of Congress.
ISBN: 978-1-4677-3860-6 (lib. bdg. : alk.
paper)
ISBN: 978-1-4677-6084-3 (pbk.)
ISBN: 978-1-4677-6262-5 (EB pdf)

Manufactured in the United States of America
1 - PC - 12/31/14

MISSISSIPPI Welcomes You!

Mississippi is full of great experiences. In the spring, the scent of magnolia flowers fills the air. The state's many forests, rivers, and beaches add up to a lot of fun. People of every age come to Mississippi for its rich history, museums, and festivals. From hiking in the Appalachian Mountain foothills to chasing waves off the Gulf Coast, there is so much to do. Read on to learn about the top ten things that make Mississippi super!

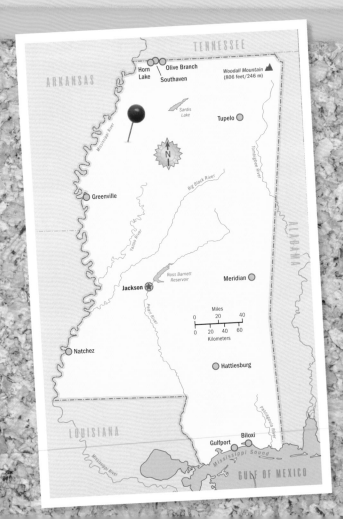

Explore Mississippi's parks and all the places in between. Just turn the page to find out all about the **MAGNOLIA STATE.** >

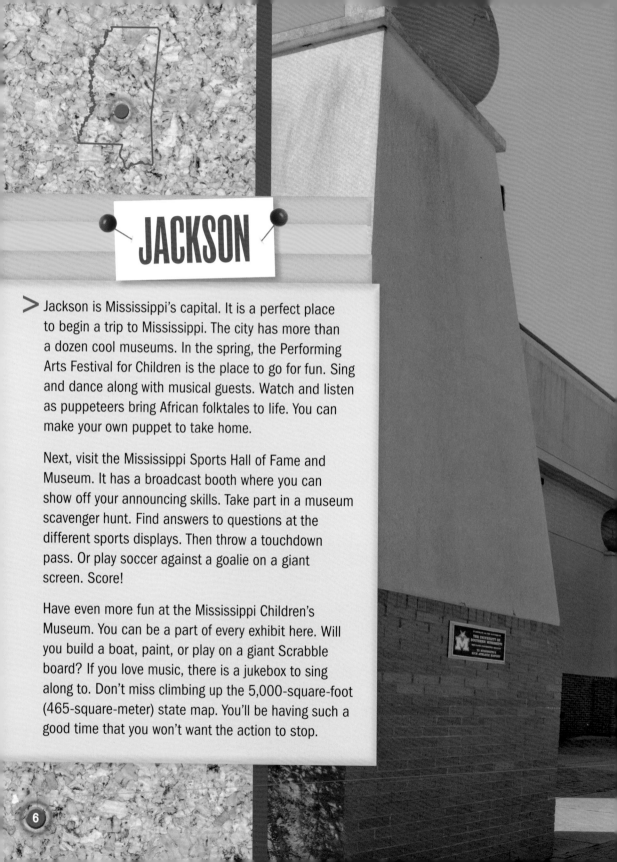

JACKSON

> Jackson is Mississippi's capital. It is a perfect place to begin a trip to Mississippi. The city has more than a dozen cool museums. In the spring, the Performing Arts Festival for Children is the place to go for fun. Sing and dance along with musical guests. Watch and listen as puppeteers bring African folktales to life. You can make your own puppet to take home.

Next, visit the Mississippi Sports Hall of Fame and Museum. It has a broadcast booth where you can show off your announcing skills. Take part in a museum scavenger hunt. Find answers to questions at the different sports displays. Then throw a touchdown pass. Or play soccer against a goalie on a giant screen. Score!

Have even more fun at the Mississippi Children's Museum. You can be a part of every exhibit here. Will you build a boat, paint, or play on a giant Scrabble board? If you love music, there is a jukebox to sing along to. Don't miss climbing up the 5,000-square-foot (465-square-meter) state map. You'll be having such a good time that you won't want the action to stop.

See historical items from local sports teams, including old footballs and photographs, at the Mississippi Sports Hall of Fame and Museum.

Spell out words and play on the giant Scrabble board at the Mississippi Children's Museum.

MISSISSIPPI
SPORTS HALL OF FAME & MUSEUM

NATCHEZ TRACE PARKWAY

> The Natchez Trace Parkway has been an important travel route for thousands of years. It runs from Natchez, Mississippi, to Nashville, Tennessee. American Indians once walked this 450-mile-long (724-kilometer) path. It's still a great scenic road for bicycling or driving.

The Trace offers many fun programs and activities. At the visitor center in Tupelo, make a plaster cast of an animal's footprint. Or learn to fight a forest fire! You can dress up as a firefighter. Then park rangers will show you how real firefighters fight forest fires. During Pioneer Days, you will see how people lived in the 1800s. You can weave a basket and make a corn husk doll. Don't leave the Trace before seeing Cypress Swamp near Jackson. Gaze up at the twisting trees. You may feel as if you have stepped inside a book of fairy tales.

TRAVELING THE TRACE

Boat operators called Kaintucks floated goods to markets down the Mississippi and Ohio Rivers during the 1800s. Their flat-bottom boats carried coal, farm crops, and animals. After everything was sold, they took apart their boats and sold the wood. Then they walked back home along the Trace. It took slightly more than one month to walk the whole path.

Make your own corn husk doll during Pioneer Days.

TISHOMINGO STATE PARK

> Tishomingo State Park is a great place for fun and adventure. This park is by the Appalachian Mountains. The Natchez Trace runs through it. See huge mossy boulders. Hike along trails American Indians once used. Later, see if you can catch a fish for lunch in Bear Creek. Cross over the creek on the swinging bridge. It was built in 1939. From here, you'll have a great view high above Bear Creek.

There's still more excitement waiting for you on Bear Creek. Sign up for a canoe trip. Canoes leave every morning. You will have tons of fun paddling down the creek. You may see a heron looking for a tasty meal. End your day with a game of disc golf on one of the three courses. The park office offers discs for free. Who in your group will win with the lowest score? If you want to stay for more than one day, the park also has camping sites for everyone to enjoy.

Watch for herons hunting for fish while you paddle down Bear Creek.

CHOCTAW, CHICKASAW, AND NATCHEZ AMERICAN INDIANS

American Indians were the first people to live in Mississippi. The three largest groups were the Choctaw, the Chickasaw, and the Natchez. The Choctaw and the Natchez were good farmers. They grew corn, beans, melons, and squash. The Natchez also built large temple mounds of dirt. These were often the bases of sacred buildings. The Natchez met at the mounds for religious ceremonies. One of the largest mounds in North America is Emerald Mound near the Natchez Trace. The Chickasaw were great hunters. They traded deerskins with Europeans who came to Mississippi in the 1600s.

MISSISSIPPI AGRICULTURE AND FORESTRY MUSEUM

> What was life like in Mississippi in the early 1900s? Jump on the Mississippi Agriculture and Forestry Museum train in Jackson to find out. This train will take you to an old-time town. Be sure to bring your camera. You can snap photos of a sawmill or America's oldest-working cotton gin. See an old gas station. Go inside the doctor's office or the schoolhouse. Can you imagine doing your homework on a tiny chalkboard called a slate?

Then visit the barnyard. Pet the goats. Or meet the mules, Joe and Sally. Chickens and peacocks also live in the barnyard. In the spring, you'll see even more on hayrides and farmhouse tours. Watch the blacksmith hard at work making horseshoes. Sparks will fly!

Next, play with model trains in the museum. Push buttons to move the trains and hear their horns and bells. End your trip at the museum café. Here, you can enjoy a southern meal of fried chicken and bread pudding.

View the oldest-working cotton gins in the United States at the Mississippi Agriculture and Forestry Museum.

Visit the National Agricultural Aviation Museum, located within the larger museum, to see old crop-dusting planes.

TUNICA RIVERPARK & MUSEUM

> Mississippi is known for its wetlands. One of the best places to enjoy them is the Tunica RiverPark in Robinsonville. You can ride a bike along the boardwalk over creeks and ponds. You may see turtles. If you are extra quiet, you might even spot a deer!

Go on a different kind of journey inside the Mississippi River Museum. Learn all about the Mississippi River. Crawl through an American Indian mound. Find arrowheads and see bone tools. Learn how to spot animals in the wild. Then hide behind logs as you look through giant binoculars or a camera lens. You will feel like a wildlife photographer.

There is even more to see inside the big aquariums. Here you will find fish, frogs, and snakes that live in the state. An alligator could even wade by. Then step inside the diving bell simulator. It's a container divers use to go underwater. It allows for a pocket of air. You will be able to tell your friends what the bottom of the Mississippi River looks like!

MISSISSIPPI RIVER

The Mississippi River is the second-longest river in America. It is 2,350 miles (3,782 km) long and flows through ten states. The river begins at Lake Itasca in Minnesota. It ends its journey at the Gulf of Mexico. The Mississippi has flooded many times in history. This led to the building of levees to control the river. Most of the rich soil in Mississippi is silt left by these floodwaters.

Keep your eyes peeled for deer as you bike along the Tunica RiverPark boardwalk.

GREAT MISSISSIPPI RIVER BALLOON RACE

> The fall skies in Natchez will take your breath away. In fall, more than one hundred colorful hot air balloons rise above the city. The Great Mississippi River Balloon Race is one of the biggest festivals in the state.

The evening before the race is the big kickoff. This is your chance to see the balloons up close. Dozens of balloons are inflated just before dark at the Rosalie Bicentennial Gardens. Some balloons are as big as ten-story buildings. Watch the balloon glow! The balloons light up like giant lanterns.

As the sun sets, make your way to the Mississippi River. A fireworks show caps off the night. The next day, visit the carnival. There's so much to see and do. Ride around on the Ferris wheel. Listen to live music. Watch balloon pilots compete in a sandbag-throwing contest. The pilots toss sandbags out of their balloons, aiming for a large target on the ground. Or try your luck at one of the carnival games. You might win a prize!

Watch fireworks explode over the Mississippi River at the Great Mississippi River Balloon Race.

Get to Rosalie Bicentennial Gardens the night before the race to watch the balloon glow.

See the USS *Cairo*, a ship built and used during the Civil War, at Vicksburg National Military Park.

VICKSBURG NATIONAL MILITARY PARK

> Step back in time at Vicksburg National Military Park. It's the site of one of the most important battles in the Civil War (1861–1865). See historic statues and monuments. A guide will take you on the battlefield tour. Or download an app and lead the way yourself.

In the summer, volunteers dress in Civil War clothing. You can join in too. Pick up a wooden musket and be part of a drill. Listen to the drums call to the soldiers on the field. *Rat-a tat-tat-tat!* You'll feel as if you're part of the battle.

While you are at the park, check out the USS *Cairo* ship and museum. This ship is a must-see! It's an ironclad gunboat that sunk in the Yazoo River. One hundred years later, it was pulled out and restored. Watch a video showing how the recovery and restoration were done.

CIVIL WAR

Before the Civil War, there was a balance between free and slave states in the United States. People in northern and southern states disagreed on the issue of slavery. Northerners wanted to ban slavery throughout the country. Southerners relied on unpaid slaves for labor on their plantations. In November 1860, Abraham Lincoln was elected president. He promised to stop slavery from spreading. South Carolina left the Union on December 20, 1860. The Union was the term used to describe the United States at the time. On January 9, 1861, Mississippi also left. Other southern states followed, and the Civil War began.

The Biloxi Lighthouse was built in 1848 and has stayed strong even through deadly hurricanes.

BILOXI

> Biloxi has been holding its Blessing of the Fleet and Shrimp Festival every May since 1929. Thousands of people come to eat seafood and listen to live music. You can see the crowning of the Shrimp King and Queen as well. The ceremony kicks off the beginning of the shrimp season.

On the festival's parade day, the waters of Mississippi Sound look like a rainbow. More than one hundred colorful shrimping boats enter the shrimp parade. Most ships are decorated with flags. Wave to the boaters as they sail by.

While in Biloxi, climb to the top of the Biloxi Lighthouse. From there, you'll have a great view of the Gulf Coast. Be sure to look toward Deer Island. People claim to see mysterious lights here. Some believe it is the ghost of an old pirate. He is said to have buried his treasure on the island.

HURRICANE KATRINA

On August 29, 2005, Hurricane Katrina hit Mississippi's Gulf Coast. This very powerful storm destroyed businesses, homes, schools, and more. Hundreds of thousands of people had to leave their homes. They were forced to live in shelters with friends or strangers. Many people died in the storm. Since then, the people of Mississippi have been working hard to rebuild the Gulf Coast region.

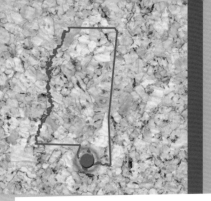

See spacecraft up close at the Infinity Science Center.

INFINITY SCIENCE CENTER

> The Infinity Science Center in Pearlington is bursting with science and space adventures. Set off on a scavenger hunt through the center's 4,000-square-foot (371 sq. m) maze. It will take you all around the world. Smell spices from Egypt. Discover which space shuttle astronaut Buzz Aldrin flew on.

Then take a seat in the Omega Flight Simulator. Hang on tight as the ride shakes you. Will you have what it takes to blast off into space? Try out the pilot's chair in the mock space shuttle. See if you can guide the ship back home. Then walk inside a model of the International Space Station. You can build your own space shuttle on a magnetic wall.

Later, see America's largest test rocket center. A bus will take you to NASA's Stennis Space Center. This is where rockets that carried astronauts to the moon were tested! You may be hungry after all that space travel. Treat yourself to some astronaut ice cream back at the center. It's ice cream that has been freeze-dried so astronauts can take it into space!

See a replica of NASA's Orion capsule in the Space Gallery.

GULFPORT

> The city of Gulfport is the perfect spot to end your Mississippi vacation. Gulfport is in the southernmost part of Mississippi. On a hot summer day, Gulf Islands Waterpark is the place to be. It is the largest water park on the coast. Grab a mat and jump onto one of the many waterslides. You will have a blast twisting and turning your way down. Or grab a tube and float along the lazy river.

After you're done exploring the water park, visit the Institute for Marine Mammal Studies in Gulfport. Pet sharks, sea urchins, and horseshoe crabs in the touch pools. Or try out the marine fossil dig. It will have you sifting sand until you find a shark tooth to bring home! Outside the center, meet the dolphins, Bo and Buster. Have you ever dreamed of working with dolphins? This is your chance! Here, you can get in the water and help them with a trick.

YOUR TOP TEN

Now that you've read about ten awesome things to see and do in Mississippi, think about what your Mississippi top ten list would include. If you were planning a Mississippi vacation, what would you like to see? Write your top ten list on a separate sheet of paper. Or turn your list into a booklet. You can add drawings or pictures from the Internet or magazines.

Grab a tube and enjoy the lazy river or the wave pool at Gulf Islands Waterpark.

Hold a spiky sea urchin at the Institute for Marine Mammal Studies.

MISSISSIPPI BY MAP

> MAP KEY

⭐ Capital city

⚪ City

⚙ Point of interest

▲ Highest elevation

–·– State border

— Natchez Trace Parkway
   (Natchez to Nashville, TN)

Visit www.lernerresource.com to learn
more about the state flag of Mississippi.

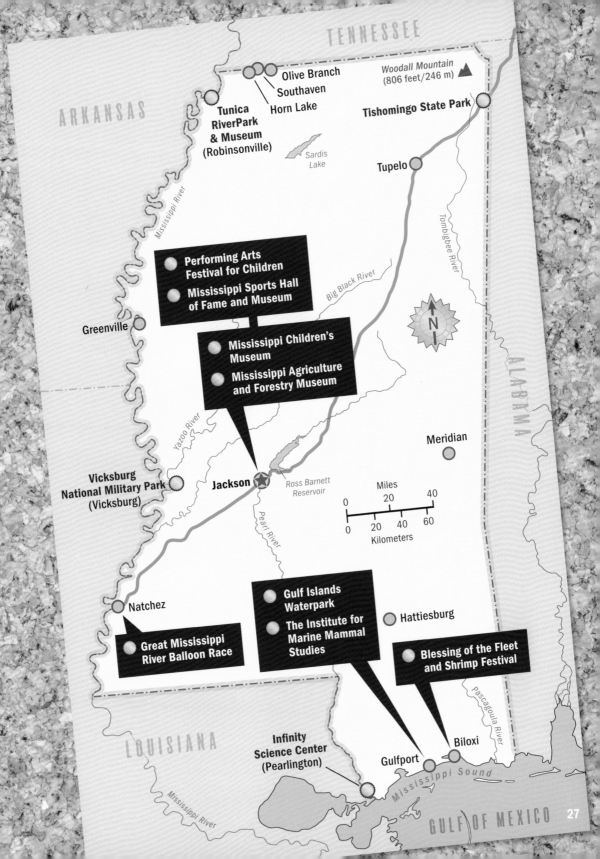

TENNESSEE

ARKANSAS

Olive Branch
Southaven
Horn Lake

Tunica
RiverPark
& Museum
(Robinsonville)

Woodall Mountain
(806 feet/246 m) ▲

Tishomingo State Park

Sardis
Lake

Tupelo

Mississippi River

Big Black River

Tombigbee River

Performing Arts
Festival for Children

Mississippi Sports Hall
of Fame and Museum

Greenville

Mississippi Children's
Museum

Mississippi Agriculture
and Forestry Museum

N

Meridian

Yazoo River

ALABAMA

Vicksburg
National Military Park
(Vicksburg)

Jackson

Ross Barnett
Reservoir

Miles

0   20   40

0   20   40   60
Kilometers

Pearl River

Natchez

Great Mississippi
River Balloon Race

Gulf Islands
Waterpark

The Institute for
Marine Mammal
Studies

Hattiesburg

Blessing of the Fleet
and Shrimp Festival

Pascagoula River

LOUISIANA

Infinity
Science Center
(Pearlington)

Gulfport

Biloxi

Mississippi Sound

Mississippi River

GULF OF MEXICO

MISSISSIPPI FACTS

NICKNAME: Magnolia State

SONG: "Go, Mis-sis-sip-pi" by Houston Davis

MOTTO: *Virtute et Armis*, or "By valor and arms"

> **FLOWER:** southern magnolia

TREE: southern magnolia

> **BIRD:** northern mockingbird

WATER MAMMAL: bottlenose dolphin

DATE AND RANK OF STATEHOOD: December 10, 1817; the 20th state

> **CAPITAL:** Jackson

AREA: 47,692 square miles (123,522 sq. km)

AVERAGE JANUARY TEMPERATURE: 46°F (8°C)

AVERAGE JULY TEMPERATURE: 81°F (27°C)

POPULATION AND RANK: 2,991,207; 31st (2013)

MAJOR CITIES AND POPULATIONS: Jackson (172,638), Gulfport (71,012), Southaven (50,997), Hattiesburg (47,556), Biloxi (44,820)

NUMBER OF US CONGRESS MEMBERS: 4 representatives; 2 senators

NUMBER OF ELECTORAL VOTES: 6

NATURAL RESOURCES: water, seafood, forestry, farmland, oil, natural gas

AGRICULTURAL PRODUCTS: catfish, cattle, eggs, corn, rice, soybeans, cotton

MANUFACTURED GOODS: petroleum and coal products, food, beverages, tobacco, chemical manufacturing, furniture, electrical equipment, transportation equipment, motor vehicle parts

HOLIDAYS AND CELEBRATIONS: Blessing of the Fleet and Shrimp Festival, Mississippi Delta Blues & Heritage Festival, Mardi Gras

GLOSSARY

agriculture: the science or occupation of raising crops and animals

blacksmith: someone who makes things by heating and bending iron

cotton gin: a machine that pulls seeds from a cotton plant

diving bell: a container used to take divers underwater

fossil: a trace of a long-ago animal or plant that is preserved as rock

hurricane: a violent and damaging storm with heavy rain and high winds

levee: a bank built up near a river to prevent flooding

mound: an American Indian structure built of soil or rocks, used for burial or other important rituals

musket: a historic gun with a long barrel used before the rifle was invented

silt: sand or mud carried by moving water

simulator: a machine that creates an imitation of how something should look or feel

LERNER

SOURCE

Expand learning beyond the printed book. Download free, complementary educational resources for this book from our website, www.lernersource.com.

FURTHER INFORMATION

Enchanted Learning—Mississippi
http://www.enchantedlearning.com/usa/states/mississippi
Learn fascinating Mississippi facts, and take a quiz about the Mississippi
state flag.

Find Your True South
http://www.governorbryant.com/wp-content/uploads/2013/03
/StudentGuide.pdf
Learn more about Mississippi's history, geography, economy, government,
and people.

Foran, Jill. *Mississippi*. Calgary: Weigl Publishers, 2013.
Learn all about the geography, the history, and the symbols of Mississippi
through maps, photographs, and easy-to-read text.

Knudsen, Shannon. *When Were the First Slaves Set Free during the Civil War?
And Other Questions about the Emancipation Proclamation.* Minneapolis:
Lerner Publications, 2011. Read about Abraham Lincoln's plan during the
Civil War to free the slaves.

Manning, Paul. *Mississippi River*. Mankato, MN: Smart Apple Media, 2015.
Find out about the cities, the dams, and the people along the Mississippi
River.

Smithsonian Channel
http://www.smithsonianchannel.com/sc/web/series/701/aerial
-america/140690/mississippi
Watch videos to learn more about the history and culture of Mississippi and
the importance of the Mississippi River.

INDEX

PHOTO ACKNOWLEDGMENTS

The images in this book are used with the permission of: © Anton Foltin/Shutterstock Images, p. 1; NASA, pp. 2–3, 22–23; © Laura Westlund/Independent Picture Service, pp. 4, 27; Carol M. Highsmith/Library of Congress, pp. 4–5 (LC-DIG-highsm-12495), 14 (LC-DIG-highsm-12794), 18–19 (LC-DIG-highsm-06780); © John Brueske/Shutterstock Images, p. 5 (top); © Don Smetzer/Alamy, pp. 6–7; © Rogelio V. Solis/AP Images, p. 7 (right), 7 (left); Jan Kronsell, p. 8; US National Park Service, pp. 8–9; John Morgan, p. 9; © Joseph Scott Photography/Shutterstock Images, p. 10; © Shutterstock Images, pp. 10–11; © John Elk III/Alamy, p. 11; © Danny Lehman/Corbis, pp. 12–13; © Stephen Saks Photography/Alamy, p. 13 (top), 13 (bottom); © Rino Dolbi/Desoto Times Today/AP Images, pp. 14–15; © Purestock/Thinkstock, p. 15; © ostill/Shutterstock Images, pp. 16–17; © Neil Lockhart/Shutterstock Images, p. 17 (bottom); © solarseven/Shutterstock Images, p. 17 (top); Mark A. Wilson, p. 18; Library of Congress, p. 19 (LC-DIG-ppmsca-35289); © Rob Hainer/Shutterstock Images, p. 20; © Goss Images/Alamy, pp. 20–21; Mark Wolfe/FEMA, p. 21; © Jim West/Alamy, pp. 22, 23; © VP Photo Studio/Shutterstock Images, pp. 24–25; © Kali Nine/iStockphoto, p. 25 (top); © NatureDiver/Shutterstock Images, p. 25 (bottom); © Nicoolay/iStockphoto, p. 26; © Lori Monahan Borden/Shutterstock Images, p. 29 (top right); © Steve Byland/Shutterstock Images, p. 29 (top left); © Katherine Welles/Shutterstock Images, p. 29 (bottom left).

Cover: © iStockphoto.com/Kresopix (swamp); © Barney Harp/Moment/Getty Images (Biloxi); © Anne Power/Dreamstime.com (balloons); © Laura Westlund/Independent Picture Service (map); © iStockphoto.com/fpm (seal); © iStockphoto.com/vicm (pushpins); © iStockphoto.com/benz190 (corkboard).